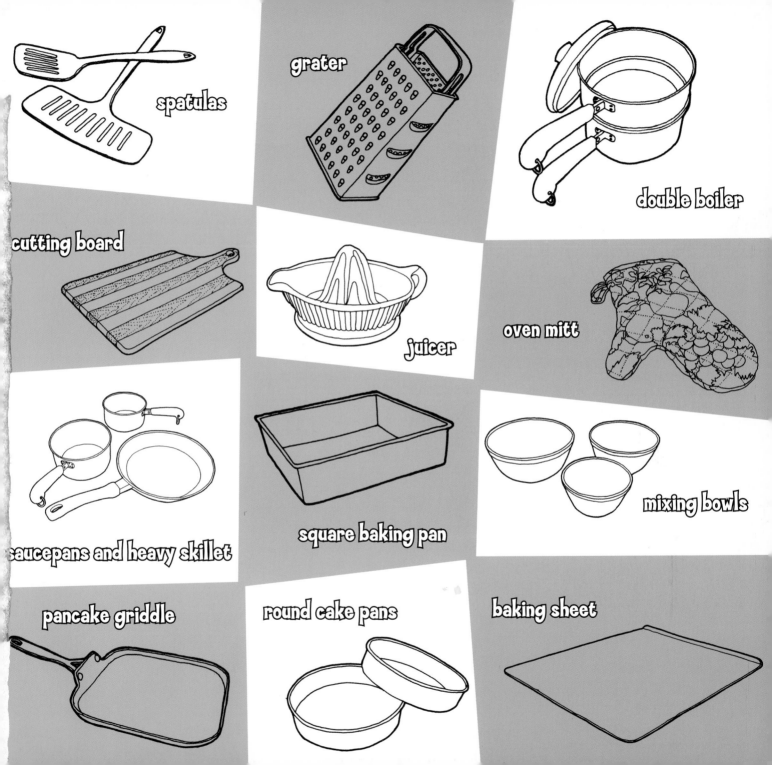

spatulas

grater

double boiler

cutting board

juicer

oven mitt

saucepans and heavy skillet

square baking pan

mixing bowls

pancake griddle

round cake pans

baking sheet

retro
kids
cooking

timeless recipes for cooks of all ages

By
Richard Perry

COLLECTORS PRESS

PORTLAND OREGON

Front Cover Design: Wade Daughtry
Book Design: Lisa M. Douglass, Collectors Press, Inc.
Editor: Sue Mann

Library of Congress Cataloging-in-Publication Data

Perry, Richard, 1960-
  Retro kids cooking : timeless recipes for cooks of all ages / Richard Perry.– 1st American ed.
      p. cm. – (Retro series)
  Includes index.
  ISBN 1-888054-96-4 (hardcover : alk. paper)
  1. Cookery. I. Title. II. Series.
  TX652.5.P48 2004
  641.5–dc22
                                    2004015593

Printed in Singapore

9 8 7 6 5 4 3 2 1

Collectors Press books are available at special discounts for bulk purchases, premiums, and promotions. Special editions, including personalized inserts or covers, and corporate logos, can be printed in quantity for special purposes. For further information contact: Special Sales, Collectors Press, Inc., P.O. Box 230986, Portland, OR 97281. Toll free: 1-800-423-1848.

Retro Kids Cooking is part of the *Retro* series by Collectors Press, Inc.

For a free catalog write: Collectors Press, Inc., P. O. Box 230986, Portland, OR 97281. Toll free: 1-800-423-1848 or visit our website at: collectorspress.com.

Dedication
This book is lovingly dedicated to my kids, Keaton and Ava.

Acknowledgements
A warm thanks to my wife, Lisa, for her long hours of help in making this book possible; my mother-in-law, W. Gail Manchur, for her guidance in crafting words; my esteemed editors, Jennifer Weaver-Neist and Sue Mann; Lisa M. Douglass at Collectors Press who designed this beautiful book; Jim Lattz for the illustrations; the daring taste-testers at Collectors Press; and my mother, Carol, for nurturing the young chef inside me.

contents

intro

When I considered writing a kids cookbook, warm childhood memories flooded back to me. I remembered the thrill of making macaroni and cheese with my mother when I was barely old enough to reach the saucepan. And later, when I was in middle school, I discovered the recipe for Dutch Baby Pancakes in my home economics class. This oven-baked classic became my weekend specialty, eagerly anticipated by my mother, in particular. The pancakes, easy enough for a kid to figure out, would change right before my eyes as I watched the heat from the oven make the edges rise like craggy rims. Out of the oven, though, the edges fell before I could pour on the syrup and float the dusting of powdered sugar. The pride I took in cooking for my family stays with me to this day. I now have children, and I'm eager to help them build their own warm kitchen memories.

For hundreds of years, the kitchen has been the focal point for family get-togethers. A few generations ago it was common for all children to actively participate in the daily preparation and presentation of meals, from harvesting vegetables to preparing and cooking them. The youngest would help wash vegetables, tear lettuce for salads, snap green beans, or even push peas out of their pods — always great fun, especially when a pea or two would escape and roll on the table or even on the floor! And children of all ages helped set the table and decorate it. They learned family recipes literally at mother's knee and by hands-on experience. Although in the years before the twentieth century it was usually the girls who helped in the kitchen, in more recent years the boys have wanted to learn how to "make stuff," and their pride in scrambled eggs, macaroni and cheese, or something more elaborate is no less than their sisters'. Today, many boys take home economics in school. Boys and girls who can prepare and serve meals use their own creativity and will experience satisfaction in a job well done — and their families will be so pleased!

The recipes gathered in this book are simple but classic. There are a few new ideas and many standard, tried-and-true favorites — and all are designed for small, inexperienced hands to conquer. I have chosen colorful, easy, tasty, and fun-sounding ingredients to peak a child's interest (*green goop* is much more interesting than *guacamole*, don't you think?). The popularity of Easy-Bake Ovens, which used the heat from a light bulb to bake tiny cakes, proved that even the youngest child, given the opportunity, will cook and bake and serve creations with confidence. If children can't cook in real kitchens, a variety of play stoves lets them serve imaginary meals. But why restrict them to pretend meals when there are so many recipes within their capabilities? To see the happiness in their own efforts is worth the time invested in supervising. I remember how much fun I had mixing pizza dough and experimenting with a variety of toppings. There is something about the feel of dough in one's hands that is a pleasure and satisfaction in itself, and children especially like to squish and squeeze it. But when I experimented with all the ingredients I could use for toppings, my efforts became my masterpiece!

There are many other advantages for children when they learn to cook. To successfully produce a meal, they must learn to plan, anticipate, deal with disappointments, and follow through to the end. They gain self-esteem and learn perseverance when they have to complete the task they started. They learn responsibility when they clean up after they are through cooking. And they learn independence if they can cook their own meals, a skill that will stand them in good stead as adults. They will always be able to produce healthy, wholesome, budget-conscious meals and won't have to live on take-out or drive-thru. And a note to teenage boys: Nothing impresses a girl so much as a meal you cook for her. It surpasses flowers, perfume, and jewelry, so it is definitely

a skill you should learn while you are still at home. And girls have always known that one of the main paths to a bachelor's heart is by way of a well-cooked, delicious meal.

I suggest starting your youngest children with easy, colorful dishes such as fruit salad, peanut butter and jelly sandwiches, or tuna fish sandwiches. Even two- or three-year-olds can put various ingredients into a bowl and stir. And they can usually manage a small spatula to smooth out the sandwich spread! As they grow older, they can take a greater role in the precooking preparation — cutting, grating, measuring, and so forth. If they can plan the menu, they can also help shop for the ingredients.

For safety's sake I suggest parental supervision on most recipes. Dishes that don't require using electric appliances or sharp kitchen tools can be prepared with minimal supervision. And I encourage you to let your children help with food presentation, setting the table and maybe decorating it with flowers (small children seem to gravitate toward dandelions in a jelly jar) or a prized toy as the centerpiece.

I guarantee that every family member will be delighted with the result, including those who only watched or supervised. And, like me, your children will always have warm, fond memories of sharing the kitchen with their parents.

Bon appetit!

classically cool snacks

chapter 1

deviled party eggs

- 6 hard-boiled eggs (12 minutes in boiling water)
- 2 tbsps mayonnaise
- 1 tsp vinegar
- pinch of salt and pepper
- paprika for garnish

Serves 6

1 Slice eggs in half lengthwise.

2 With a teaspoon remove egg yolks and place in a bowl. Mash yolks.

3 Mix in mayonnaise, vinegar, salt, and pepper.

4 With a small spoon, fill the egg white halves with yolk mixture. Sprinkle paprika on eggs. Chill and serve.

fruity freeze

- 12 oz. strawberries, fresh or frozen and thawed
- 8 oz. pineapple, fresh or canned, crushed and drained
- 1 cup (8 oz.) strawberry yogurt
- 1/4 cup powdered sugar, sifted

Serves 4 to 6

1 Mash strawberries with a fork and mix in pineapple, yogurt, and sugar.

2 Line a shallow rectangle pan with foil and pour in the fruit mixture. Freeze until firm, about three to four hours.

3 Lift foil from tray and let rest a few minutes to soften the fruit mixture. Cut mixture into squares and serve in small cups.

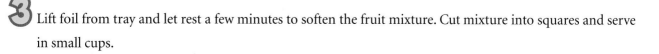

tater salad

Serves 6 to 8

- [ ] 6 medium potatoes
- [ ] 3 hard-boiled eggs, chopped
     (12 minutes in boiling water)
- [ ] 1 cup celery, chopped
- [ ] 1/2 cup black olives, chopped or sliced
- [ ] 2 tbsps green onion, chopped
- [ ] 1 cup mayonnaise
- [ ] 1/8 cup prepared mustard
- [ ] 1/4 cup dill relish
- [ ] 1/4 cup sweet relish
- [ ] salt and pepper to taste

Note: You can make this the day before and refrigerate it overnight.

1 In a covered pot, boil potatoes in their jackets. Let cool. Peel and chop into medium-to-small chunks.

2 Place potato chunks, eggs, celery, olives, and green onion in a large bowl.

3 Mix together mayonnaise, mustard, relishes, salt, and pepper.

4 Add to potato mixture and mix well.

chubby celery

- celery stalks
- cream cheese, softened, or peanut butter
- paprika (optional)

1 Wash celery, separate ribs, and cut to even lengths.

2 In a small bowl, mash cream cheese with the back of a spoon until smooth.

3 Fill celery ribs with cream cheese, peanut butter, or some of both.

4 Sprinkle cream cheese with paprika for color, if using.

Makes 1 to 2 stalks per person

snickersnack

- 4 cups Cheerios-type cereal
- 1/2 cup salted peanuts
- 1 cup golden raisins
- 1/4 cup (1/2 stick) butter
- 1 pkg (6 oz.) semisweet chocolate bits

1 Mix together cereal, peanuts, and raisins.

2 Melt butter over low heat and pour over cereal mix, mixing well.

3 Add chocolate bits, toss together, and serve.

Serves 6 to 8

green goop
(guacamole)

- [ ] 2 ripe avocados, peeled, seeds removed
- [ ] 1 small onion, chopped fine
- [ ] 1 small tomato, diced
- [ ] 1 fresh lime, juiced
- [ ] salt and pepper to taste
- [ ] tortilla chips

Serves 4 to 6

1 Scoop out avocados with a spoon and mash with a fork.

2 Add onion, tomato, lime juice, salt, and pepper. Mix well.

3 Chill and serve with tortilla chips.

nuts and bolts

- ☐ **1 cup Kix-type cereal**
- ☐ **1 cup Cheerios-type cereal**
- ☐ **1 cup thin pretzel sticks**
- ☐ **1/2 cup salted peanuts or mixed nuts**
- ☐ **3 tbsps butter**
- ☐ **1/4 tsp Worcestershire sauce**
- ☐ **1/4 tsp garlic salt**
- ☐ **1/8 tsp celery salt**

1 Heat oven to 250 degrees.

2 Mix cereals, pretzels, and nuts.

3 In a small saucepan melt butter.

4 Stir in Worcestershire sauce, garlic salt, and celery salt.

5 Pour butter mixture over cereal mixture and mix well.

6 Bake 30 minutes, stirring occasionally. Remember to use oven mitts when removing pan from oven.

Makes 3 cups

quick-energy pickups

- ☐ 4 squares of graham crackers (see Note)
- ☐ 1 cup powdered sugar
- ☐ 1 cup crunchy peanut butter
- ☐ 1 cup semisweet chocolate bits
- ☐ 1/2 cup instant nonfat dry milk
- ☐ 3 tbsps water

Makes 12 to 15 balls

Note: In place of graham crackers, you can use 1/2 cup prepared graham cracker crumbs or 2/3 cup flaked coconut.

1 Finely crumble graham crackers onto a sheet of wax paper.

2 Mix remaining ingredients in a bowl.

3 Roll the mixture into 1-inch balls. Roll balls in the graham cracker crumbs until coated.

4 Arrange the coated balls on an ungreased baking sheet and refrigerate about 20 minutes or until firm.

potato chip dip

- 8 oz. cream cheese
- 2 tbsps milk
- 2 tbsps French dressing
- 1/3 cup catsup
- 1/4 tsp salt
- 3 drops hot sauce
- potato chips or crackers

1. Soften and smooth cream cheese with a spoon.

2. Add milk and mix well.

3. Add French dressing, catsup, salt, and hot sauce and mix well.

4. Serve with potato chips, crackers, or both.

Serves 4

crunchy apple treat

- 1/2 cup applesauce
- 1/4 cup walnuts, chopped
- 4 frozen waffles or bread slices
- 1 tsp butter or margarine

1. Mix applesauce and walnuts in a small bowl.

2. Toast waffles or bread.

3. Spread with butter or margarine.

4. Spread with apple-nut mixture and serve while still warm.

make a meal

chapter

2

make a meal

breakfast boosters

egg-in-a-bun sandwiches

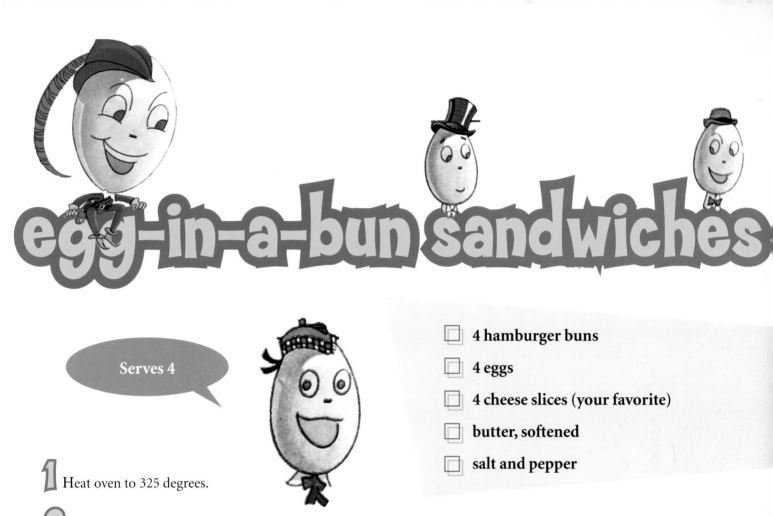

Serves 4

- ☐ **4 hamburger buns**
- ☐ **4 eggs**
- ☐ **4 cheese slices (your favorite)**
- ☐ **butter, softened**
- ☐ **salt and pepper**

1 Heat oven to 325 degrees.

2 Put a biscuit cutter in the center of a closed hamburger bun. Cut into the bun 1 inch. Don't cut through the bottom of the bun. Repeat with all the buns.

3 Carefully lift the bun circles out with a fork. Butter inside of each hole well.

4 Place buns on a baking sheet. Break an egg into each bun hole. Season with salt and pepper.

5 Bake 25 minutes. Remove from oven and top each sandwich with a slice of cheese. Bake 5 more minutes. Remember to use oven mitts when removing baking sheet from oven.

log cabin toast

- [ ] 1/4 cup sugar
- [ ] 2 tsps cinnamon
- [ ] 2 slices white or whole wheat bread
- [ ] butter, softened

Serves 1 to 2

1 In a custard cup mix together sugar and cinnamon.

2 Toast bread, spread with butter, and sprinkle with the sugar-cinnamon mixture.

3 Cut each slice of toast into four strips. Lay two strips side by side and lay two more to make a square; stack the ends on top of each other like logs of a cabin. Start from the top and eat all the logs.

french toast

- [ ] 2 eggs
- [ ] 1/2 tsp salt
- [ ] 1/8 tsp nutmeg
- [ ] 4 tbsps sugar
- [ ] 3/4 cup milk
- [ ] 1 tbsp butter
- [ ] 6 to 8 slices white bread
- [ ] butter and syrup

Serves 4 to 6

1. With a fork lightly beat the eggs, salt, nutmeg, sugar, and milk until well mixed.

2. In a frying pan melt butter until it begins to brown.

3. Dip each slice of bread in the egg batter until it is well soaked and place it in the frying pan.

4. Cook one side until lightly browned; turn over to brown the other side.

5. Keep the French toast in a warm oven until you've cooked all the bread. Serve hot with butter and syrup.

dutch baby pancakes

Serves 2 to 3

- ☐ **5 tbsps butter**
- ☐ **4 eggs**
- ☐ **1/2 tsp salt**
- ☐ **3/4 cup flour**
- ☐ **3/4 cup milk**
- ☐ **syrup, jam, or powdered sugar**
- ☐ **1 lemon (optional)**

1 Preheat oven to 425 degrees and pull out two round glass pans.

2 Divide butter into two chunks and place one in each pan. Set pans in the oven while it preheats.

3 Mix eggs, salt, flour, and milk until thoroughly blended.

4 Take the pans out of the oven and remember to use oven mitts when doing so.

5 Pour half of the batter into each pan and put them back in the oven to bake on the lowest shelf.

6 Bake for 15 minutes and serve right away with syrup, jam, or powdered sugar and a slice of lemon.

pancakes

- ☐ **1 1/4 cups flour**
- ☐ **2 1/2 tsps baking powder**
- ☐ **3/4 tsp salt**
- ☐ **1 tbsp sugar**
- ☐ **1 egg**
- ☐ **1 1/4 cups milk**
- ☐ **3 tbsps butter, melted**
- ☐ **butter and syrup**

Serves 2 to 3

1 In a medium bowl sift together flour, baking powder, salt, and sugar. Separately beat together egg, milk, and melted butter.

2 Slowly pour the liquid into the flour mixture and stir just until mixed. Batter will be slightly lumpy.

3 Heat the frying pan until hot but not smoking and spoon 1 tablespoon of batter for each pancake into the pan.

4 When bubbles appear on pancakes, turn them over to brown the other side.

5 Keep the pancakes in a warm oven until you've cooked enough for everyone. Serve with butter and syrup.

Serves 2 to 3

blueberry pancakes

☐ **pancake batter (see recipe on page 27)**

☐ **1/2 pint blueberries**

☐ **butter and syrup**

1 Make the pancake batter and cook the pancakes.

2 When bubbles appear sprinkle about eight blueberries on each pancake.

3 Turn the pancakes over and cook the other side until golden brown.

4 Serve with butter and syrup.

scrambled eggs and bacon breakfast

1 In a frying pan cook bacon over medium heat.

2 When bacon is crisp on one side, turn and fry the other side. Drain on paper towels and keep in a warm oven. Leave remaining grease in the pan for cooking eggs.

3 In a medium bowl mix together eggs, milk, and salt; beat well.

4 Make sure bacon grease covers the bottom of the pan completely.

5 Pour in egg mixture and add cheese and onion, if desired. Cook slowly, turning gently with a broad spatula as mixture starts to set at bottom of pan.

6 Serve when eggs are cooked through but still moist and shiny. Don't forget the bacon!

Serves 2

- ☐ **6 to 8 bacon slices**
- ☐ **2 eggs**
- ☐ **2 tbsps milk**
- ☐ **1/8 tsp salt**
- ☐ **2 tbsps cheese (optional)**
- ☐ **1/2 tsp minced onion (optional)**

baked eggs

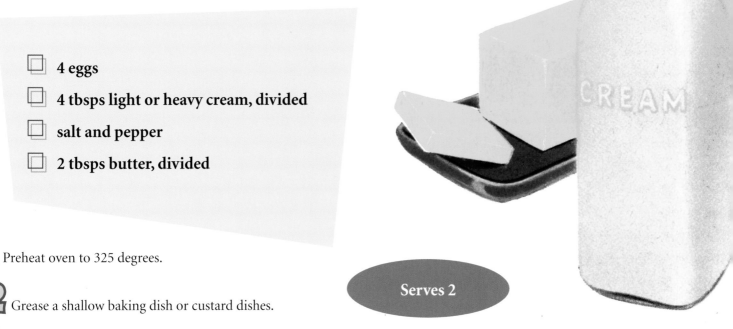

- ☐ **4 eggs**
- ☐ **4 tbsps light or heavy cream, divided**
- ☐ **salt and pepper**
- ☐ **2 tbsps butter, divided**

Serves 2

1 Preheat oven to 325 degrees.

2 Grease a shallow baking dish or custard dishes.

3 Break one egg into each custard dish or all eggs into a baking dish. Be careful to keep yolks unbroken.

4 Measure and add 1 tablespoon cream to the top of each egg. Sprinkle with salt and pepper. Using a knife, place three small bits of butter, about the size of a dime, on each egg. Cover with aluminum foil.

5 Place in oven and bake 12-18 minutes, depending on how hard-cooked you like your eggs.

6 Remove from oven and serve on plates. Remember to use oven mitts when removing dish from oven.

eggs in tomatoes

- ☐ **tomatoes, one per person**
- ☐ **salt and pepper, divided**
- ☐ **eggs, one per person**
- ☐ **bread crumbs**
- ☐ **butter**

1 Preheat oven to 350 degrees.

2 Cut the tops off tomatoes and scoop out the insides.

3 Place tomatoes in an ovenproof dish and sprinkle the insides with salt and pepper.

4 Crack an egg and drop it into the first tomato. Repeat until you have dropped an egg into each tomato.

5 Sprinkle lightly with salt and pepper.

6 Cover egg completely with bread crumbs and top with a small piece of butter.

7 Bake until the white of the egg is firm, about 15 minutes, and serve quickly. Remember to use oven mitts when removing dish from oven.

Makes 1 per person

potato egg scramble

- ☐ 3 slices bacon
- ☐ 1 pkg (5 1/2 oz.) hash browns
     with onions
- ☐ 1 3/4 cups water
- ☐ 1 1/2 tsps salt, divided
- ☐ 4 eggs
- ☐ dash of pepper

Serves 2 to 3

1 In a frying pan cook bacon over medium heat.

2 When bacon is crisp on one side, turn and fry the other side. Drain bacon on paper towels. Spoon out and throw away most of the grease, leaving just enough to cover the bottom of the pan.

3 In the same pan mix the hash browns with water and 1 teaspoon salt. Cook uncovered over medium heat until the liquid is absorbed and the bottom of the potatoes are golden brown. (Lift the edge with spatula and peek.) Turn the potatoes with the pancake turner.

4 While the potatoes are cooking, beat together eggs, remaining 1/2 teaspoon salt, and pepper.

5 Pour the egg mixture over the potatoes. Cook and stir until the eggs are thick but still moist.

6 Serve with bacon.

- [ ] 4 tbsps butter, melted and divided
- [ ] 2 tbsps brown sugar
- [ ] 12 cherries (candied or maraschino)
- [ ] 1/4 cup plus 3 tbsps chopped nuts, divided
- [ ] 1/2 cup sugar
- [ ] 1 tsp cinnamon
- [ ] 2/3 cup milk
- [ ] 2 cups Bisquick-type biscuit mix

jolly breakfast ring

Serves 4 to 6

1 Heat oven to 400 degrees.

2 Put 2 tablespoons butter in bottom of 9-inch ring mold.

3 Sprinkle in brown sugar, cherries, and 1/4 cup chopped nuts.

4 In a small bowl mix 1/2 cup sugar, cinnamon, and remaining 3 tablespoons chopped nuts.

5 In another bowl stir milk into biscuit mix. Beat 15 strokes. Dough will be stiff but sticky.

6 Shape dough into 12 balls. Roll each ball in remaining 2 tablespoons butter. Then roll in cinnamon mixture. Place balls in ring mold.

7 Bake 25-30 minutes. Turn upside down onto a plate while warm. Remember to use oven mitts when removing ring mold from oven. Serve warm.

make a meal

love
that
lunch

grilled cheese sandwich

- [ ] 1 slice processed cheese
- [ ] 2 slices light or dark bread, or 1 slice each
- [ ] 1 tbsp butter or margarine

Serves 1

Note: For variation, spread bread with mustard before adding cheese.

1. Put the cheese between the slices of bread.

2. Melt butter or margarine in a skillet over low heat. Toast sandwich in butter until sandwich is lightly browned. Watch carefully so it doesn't burn. Peek at the underside by lifting with a spatula.

3. Turn over the sandwich with the spatula. Take your time; do it carefully. Toast sandwich until the bottom side is as brown as the top side. Cut sandwich in half before serving.

grilled peanut butter sandwich

1. On one slice of bread, spread peanut butter. Add your favorite jam or jelly, or skip the jelly and add a thin slice of boiled ham, if desired.

2. On remaining slice of bread, spread softened butter.

3. Place frying pan over medium heat. Add a small amount of butter to cover the bottom of the pan, enough so that sandwich will not stick.

4. Fry on one side until golden. Turn with spatula and fry on other side.

Serves 1

☐ **2 slices bread**
☐ **butter, softened, plus more for pan**
☐ **peanut butter**
☐ **jelly or ham slice (optional)**

tuna fish boats

- [ ] 1 can (6 1/2 or 7 oz.) tuna fish
- [ ] 1/2 cup celery, chopped
- [ ] 1/4 cup mayonnaise, or bottled
      lemon juice and softened butter
- [ ] long rolls like hot dog buns or hero
      rolls, uncut
- [ ] parsley (optional)

Fish is Thrifty!
Fish is Nifty...

Serves 4 to 5

1 Open tuna fish and drain liquid through strainer directly into sink.

2 When chopping celery, hold stalk at leafy end on a chopping board.
Slice lengthwise with paring knife to about 1 inch from end. Slice crosswise.

3 In bowl combine tuna, celery, and mayonnaise or lemon juice and butter.

4 Prepare boats by hollowing inside of each bun (leaving 1/2-inch shell) with a grapefruit knife
It has a curved blade.

5 Fill boats with tuna mixture. Decorate with a sprig of parsley, if desired.

silhouette sandwiches

Serves 4 to 6

☐ **butter**

☐ **8 slices bread**

☐ **8 slices cold luncheon meat**

☐ **4 slices processed American cheese**

1 Butter top side of each slice of bread.

2 Top each with a slice of meat. Set aside.

3 With a cookie cutter of your choice, cut out the center of each slice of cheese. Separate the four cut-out middles and the four edges on two separate pieces of wax paper. Avoid stacking the cheese, as the pieces might stick together.

4 Top each meat slice with a cheese cut-out or cheese edge so the meat shows through the space in the cheese, making a silhouette.

fruit fried sandwich

- [ ] 2 slices bread
- [ ] butter, divided
- [ ] grape, strawberry, or other jelly
- [ ] 1/2 medium apple, cored and peeled

Serves 1

OH, BOY...
WHAT A
SANDWICH!

1 Spread butter thinly on one slice of bread.

2 Cover with jelly.

3 Grate the apple finely over the jelly.

4 Cover with the second slice of bread.

5 In a frying pan, fry lightly in butter on both sides until golden brown.

6 Serve hot, but remember: HOT JELLY CAN EASILY BURN YOUR TONGUE.

sunshine sandwiches

- 1/4 cup frozen orange juice concentrate, undiluted
- 1/2 cup peanut butter
- 8 slices bread

Serves 4

1 In a small bowl mix the orange juice concentrate and peanut butter with a fork until well blended.

2 Spread the peanut butter mixture on four slices of bread.

3 Top with remaining four slices, cut each sandwich in half, and serve with a sunshiny smile.

banana butter sandwich

Serves 2

- 4 slices bread
- peanut butter
- 1 ripe banana
- butter

1 Spread peanut butter on two slices of bread.

2 Slice bananas and place slices on peanut butter.

3 Butter the two remaining slices of bread and place buttered side down over the bananas. Eat right away. (Bananas turn brown quickly once you peel them.)

cowboy's standby sandwich

- ☐ 1 tbsp butter
- ☐ 1/4 cup minced onion
- ☐ 2 tbsps minced green pepper
- ☐ 4 eggs
- ☐ 1/2 cup cooked ham, cubed
- ☐ 1/4 cup milk
- ☐ 1/2 tsp salt
- ☐ 1/2 tsp pepper
- ☐ bread or hot buttered toast

1. In a small frying pan melt butter.

2. Add onion and green pepper.

3. Fry slowly until onion is transparent, stirring occasionally.

4. Remove from heat.

5. Break eggs into a bowl.

6. Stir in ham, milk, salt, and pepper; beat well with a fork.

7. Pour egg mixture into frying pan and cook over low heat.

8. Cook slowly, turning gently with a broad spatula as mixture starts to set at bottom of pan.

9. When eggs are cooked through but are still moist and shiny, spoon between slices of bread or hot buttered toast.

red robin

- [ ] **1 can tomato soup (undiluted)**
- [ ] **1 cup American cheese, grated**
- [ ] **1 egg, beaten**
- [ ] **dash salt and pepper**
- [ ] **4 slices hot toast**

1 In the top of a double boiler, mix the soup and cheese and cook slowly until cheese melts.

2 Add egg, salt, and pepper.

3 Serve over hot toast.

Serves 2 to 4

little pizzas

Serves 2 to 3

- [ ] **2 English muffins**
- [ ] **1/4 cup catsup**
- [ ] **1/4 cup American cheese, grated**
- [ ] **1 hot dog**

1 Preheat the broiler.

2 Split muffins in half and toast them in the toaster.

3 Spread each toasted muffin half with catsup, then sprinkle cheese on top.

4 Slice hot dogs into coin-size pieces and place a few on top of each muffin.

5 Place pizzas on broiler pan.

6 Broil 1 minute, until cheese is melted. Remember to use oven mitts when removing pan from oven.

chicken-apple salad

1 Drain cans of chicken well and place chicken in a bowl.

2 Add chopped celery to the chicken.

3 Wash and dry apples. Do not peel them. Cut out the cores and throw away; chop apples into 1-inch pieces. Add to chicken and celery.

4 Pour lemon juice over chicken mixture.

5 Cut grapes in half and mix with chicken mixture.

6 Add mayonnaise and stir well. Cover the bowl with a plate or aluminum foil and put into the refrigerator at least 1 hour before serving.

7 Wash and dry lettuce leaves.

8 Put one lettuce leaf on each plate. Pile salad on top of each leaf and serve.

- 2 5-oz. cans boned chicken
- 1 cup (3 stalks) celery, without leaves, chopped
- 2 red apples, unpeeled
- 2 tbsps frozen lemon juice, diluted
- 1 cup fresh seedless grapes
- 1/2 cup mayonnaise
- 4 large lettuce leaves

Serves 4

hamburgers

- ☐ **1 pound ground chuck**
- ☐ **salt**
- ☐ **pepper**
- ☐ **4 hamburger buns**
- ☐ **mustard and catsup**

1 Put the ground chuck in a bowl and break up with a fork.

2 Add salt and pepper.

3 Form into four patties with your hands. Wash your hands.

4 Broil patties about 3 inches from the heat for 6 minutes on one side. Then turn over and broil another 6 minutes.

5 Put each pattie into a bun. Serve with mustard and catsup.

Serves 4

sloppy joes

- [ ] 1 celery stalk, without leaves
- [ ] 1 pound ground beef
- [ ] 3 tbsps instant minced onion
- [ ] 1 tsp salt
- [ ] 1/8 tsp pepper
- [ ] 1 jar (about 16 oz.) spaghetti sauce
- [ ] 6 to 8 hamburger buns

1 Wash celery and chop into 1/2-inch pieces.

2 Crumble meat into skillet. Cook and stir over medium-high heat until meat is brown on all sides, about 10 minutes. Spoon out any fat and throw it away.

3 Stir celery, onion, salt, pepper, and spaghetti sauce into the meat. Heat to boiling, stirring constantly. Reduce heat to low and simmer uncovered 10 minutes, stirring occasionally.

4 Cut hamburger buns in half horizontally and place cut sides up on an ungreased baking sheet. Heat oven to broil or 550 degrees.

5 Toast the buns until light brown, about 1 to 2 minutes; watch carefully so they don't burn.

6 Place buns on plates. Remember to use oven mitts when removing baking sheet from oven.

7 Spoon the meat mixture onto bottom half of each bun and cover with top half.

Serves 6 to 8

all-american hot dogs

Serves 4

- [ ] 2 cups water
- [ ] 2 hot dogs
- [ ] 2 hot dog rolls
- [ ] mustard and catsup

1 In a medium saucepan heat water to boiling.

2 Using tongs, place hot dogs into the boiling water very carefully. Be careful not to pierce the skins.

3 Turn off the heat and leave the hot dogs in the hot water 5 minutes.

4 Slit the side of each hot dog roll lengthwise. Using tongs, remove hot dogs from water and place each hot dog inside each hot dog roll.

5 Serve with mustard and catsup.

hot dog special

- [ ] 4 hot dogs
- [ ] 4 slices bacon
- [ ] 4 slices American cheese
- [ ] 8 toothpicks (wooden)

1 Heat oven to 400 degrees.

2 Split the hot dogs lengthwise, but do not slice all the way through. Stack cheese slices and cut into eight wedges.

3 Stuff the cheese wedges into the hot dogs and wrap a slice of bacon around the hot dogs to hold in the cheese.

4 Fasten the ends of the bacon with toothpicks.

5 Bake on a baking sheet until bacon is crisp. Remember to use oven mitts when removing baking sheet from oven.

Serves 2

speedy chili

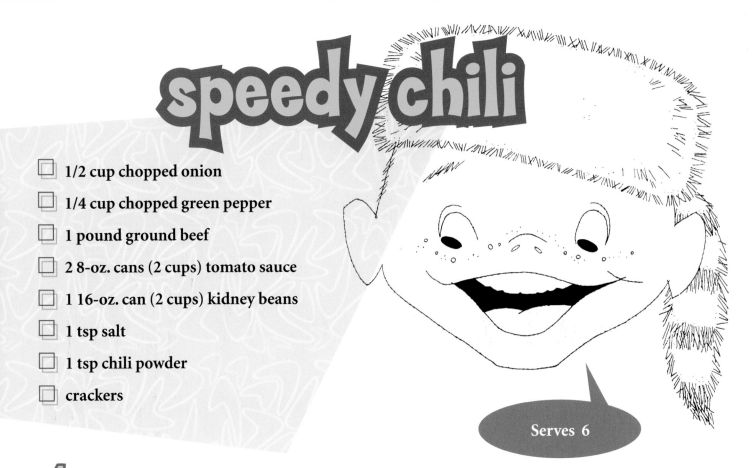

- [ ] 1/2 cup chopped onion
- [ ] 1/4 cup chopped green pepper
- [ ] 1 pound ground beef
- [ ] 2 8-oz. cans (2 cups) tomato sauce
- [ ] 1 16-oz. can (2 cups) kidney beans
- [ ] 1 tsp salt
- [ ] 1 tsp chili powder
- [ ] crackers

Serves 6

1 In a medium saucepan cook together onion, green pepper, and beef until beef is lightly browned. Spoon off excess fat and throw it away.

2 Stir in tomato sauce; cook over low heat 5 minutes.

3 Stir in kidney beans and salt. Cook until heated through.

4 Stir in chili powder. Taste and add a little more if you like it zippy.

5 Serve with crackers.

easy spaghetti

- ☐ 1 tbsp salad oil
- ☐ 1 onion, chopped
- ☐ 1/2 pound ground beef
- ☐ 1/2 tsp salt
- ☐ 1 15 1/2-oz. can spaghetti in
  tomato sauce

Serves 3 to 4

1 In a frying pan heat the oil and cook the onion until tender but not browned.

2 Add the beef and cook, stirring until brown.

3 Add the salt and spaghetti.

4 Cook until heated through.

 49

swedish meat balls

Serves 6

1 In a frying pan melt butter.

2 Add green pepper and onion; cook until tender.

3 Stir in soups and water or beef stock.

4 Heat to boiling, then turn down heat.

5 In a bowl put bread pieces, evaporated milk, egg, salt, and beef.

6 Mix thoroughly and shape into balls about the size of a ping pong ball. Drop balls into simmering sauce and cook slowly, about 1 hour, or until sauce has thickened.

- [ ] **1 tbsp butter**
- [ ] **1 green pepper, chopped**
- [ ] **1 onion, minced**
- [ ] **1 10 1/2-oz. can condensed chicken with rice soup**
- [ ] **1 10 1/2-oz. can condensed tomato soup**
- [ ] **1 cup water or beef stock**
- [ ] **2 slices soft bread, broken in pieces**
- [ ] **1/4 cup evaporated milk**
- [ ] **1 egg**
- [ ] **1 tsp salt**
- [ ] **1 pound ground beef**

polka-dotted macaroni and cheese

- ☐ **1 pkg (7 oz.) macaroni**
- ☐ **1 10 1/2-oz. can cheddar cheese soup**
- ☐ **1/2 cup milk**
- ☐ **1 tsp Worcestershire sauce (optional)**
- ☐ **2 hot dogs**

Serves 4 to 6

1. Heat oven to 375 degrees.

2. Cook macaroni as directed on package and drain.

3. Empty soup into a bowl.

4. Slowly stir in milk and Worcestershire sauce, if desired.

5. Spread drained macaroni in a 10 x 6 x 1 1/2-inch baking dish.

6. Pour cheese soup mixture over macaroni, stirring to mix.

7. Cut hot dogs into penny-thin slices.

8. Arrange frankfurter slices on top of macaroni and cheese.

9. Bake 25 minutes or until mixture is hot and bubbly. Remember to use oven mitts when removing dish from oven.

hot diggity dog pizza

Serves 8

- ☐ **2 cups Bisquick-type biscuit mix**
- ☐ **1/2 cup water**
- ☐ **1 5 1/2-oz. can (2/3 cup) pizza sauce**
- ☐ **4 hot dogs**
- ☐ **1/2 cup processed American cheese, shredded**
- ☐ **1/4 cup pickle relish**
- ☐ **3 green pepper rings**

1. Heat oven to 425 degrees.

2. In a small bowl mix together biscuit mix and water.

3. On a floured surface shape dough into a ball and knead six times (fold, turn, press dough with heel of hand).

4. Roll into a 13-inch circle about 1/4-inch thick.

5. Place crust on round pizza pan; pinch edges to make rim.

6. Pour sauce on crust.

7. Cut hot dogs into thin slices.

8. Top pizza with hot dog slices, cheese, and relish.

9. Bake until crust edge is golden brown, about 15 minutes. Remember to use oven mitts when removing pan from oven.

10. Top with green pepper rings.

11. Cut into eight pieces with a pizza cutter.

pigs in blankets

1 Heat oven to 450 degrees.

2 In a medium bowl mix together biscuit mix and milk to form a soft dough.

3 Beat vigorously for 20 strokes until dough is stiff and slightly sticky.

4 Place dough on a lightly floured board to prevent sticking.

5 Knead dough gently by folding, pressing, and turning.

6 Repeat 8-10 times to smooth the dough.

- [ ] **2 cups Bisquick-type biscuit mix**
- [ ] **2/3 cup milk**
- [ ] **12 hot dogs**

7 With lightly floured rolling pin, roll dough into a square about 12 x 12 inches.

8 Cut dough into 12 oblong shapes, each 4 inches long and 3 inches wide.

9 Wrap each hotdog in an oblong of dough. The ends of the hot dog will peek out of the biscuit "blanket."

Serves 8 to 12

10 Place on an ungreased baking sheet.

11 Bake 15 minutes. Remember to use oven mitts when removing baking sheet from oven. Serve hot.

meat loaf

1 Heat oven to 350 degrees.

2 Put all ingredients into a large bowl and mix thoroughly with a wooden spoon.

3 Line a medium-sized loaf pan with heavy wax paper. (This makes it easier to take the baked meat loaf out of the pan, and the pan is easier to clean, too!). Spread meat mixture in pan.

4 Place loaf pan in the center of the oven for even baking.

5 Bake 60 minutes. Remember to use oven mitts when removing pan from oven.

6 Let meat loaf sit covered for about 10 minutes.

7 Turn meat loaf onto platter and remove wax paper.

Serves 4 to 6

- ☐ 2/3 cup evaporated milk, undiluted
- ☐ 1 egg
- ☐ 1/2 cup cracker crumbs
- ☐ 1 1/2 pounds ground beef
- ☐ 1 1/2 tsps salt
- ☐ 1 1/2 tsps pepper
- ☐ 1 tsp dry mustard
- ☐ 1/4 cup onion, chopped
- ☐ 1/2 cup green pepper, chopped

oven-fried chicken

1 Heat oven to 375 degrees.

2 In a skillet melt butter over low heat; remove from heat.

3 Before opening the package of potato chips, crush the package with a rolling pin to crush the chips.

4 In a bowl combine potato chips with garlic salt and pepper.

5 Dip chicken pieces in melted butter, then roll in potato chip mixture.

6 Place chicken in a baking pan, skin side up.

7 Pour any remaining melted butter and potato chip mixture over chicken.

8 Bake 1 hour. Remember to use oven mitts when removing pan from oven.

9 Use tongs to remove chicken from the pan and place in a colorful, napkin-lined basket for serving at the table.

Serves 4

- ☐ **1/2 cup butter**
- ☐ **1 4-oz. pkg potato chips**
- ☐ **1/4 tsp garlic salt**
- ☐ **dash pepper**
- ☐ **1 2 1/2- to 3-pound, ready-to-cook broiler-fryer chicken, cut up**

glazed chicken drumsticks

- 3 pounds chicken drumsticks
- 3 tbsps soy sauce
- 2 tbsps honey
- 1 tbsp salad oil
- 1 tbsp chili sauce
- 1/2 tsp salt
- 1/4 tsp ginger
- 1/8 tsp garlic powder

1 Wash the drumsticks and pat dry with paper towels. Place in ungreased baking dish.

2 With a fork mix remaining ingredients in a bowl and pour over the drumsticks.

3 Cover the baking dish with aluminum foil and refrigerate at least 1 hour.

4 Heat oven to 375 degrees.

Serves 6 to 8

5 With tongs, lift the drumsticks onto a rack in a broiler pan. Brush the drumsticks with the sauce remaining in the baking dish.

6 Bake 50 to 60 minutes or until the drumsticks are tender when pierced with a fork. Remember to use oven mitts when removing pan from oven.

tuna and chips casserole

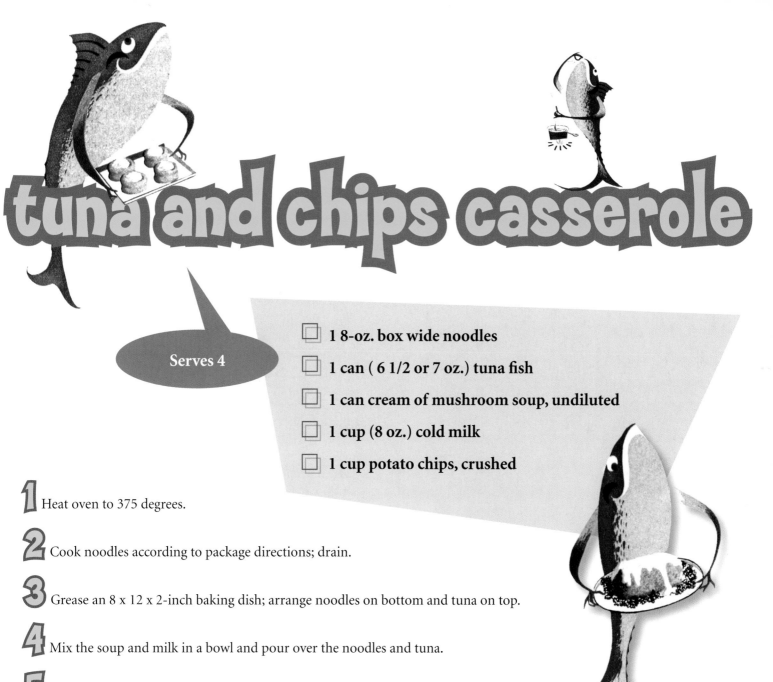

Serves 4

- [ ] 1 8-oz. box wide noodles
- [ ] 1 can (6 1/2 or 7 oz.) tuna fish
- [ ] 1 can cream of mushroom soup, undiluted
- [ ] 1 cup (8 oz.) cold milk
- [ ] 1 cup potato chips, crushed

1 Heat oven to 375 degrees.

2 Cook noodles according to package directions; drain.

3 Grease an 8 x 12 x 2-inch baking dish; arrange noodles on bottom and tuna on top.

4 Mix the soup and milk in a bowl and pour over the noodles and tuna.

5 Sprinkle potato chips over the top and bake 25 to 30 minutes until nicely browned. Remember to use oven mitts when removing dish from oven.

hawaiian thinga kabobs

- [ ] 1 8 oz. can chopped ham
- [ ] 1 8 oz. can pineapple chunks
- [ ] 1 green pepper
- [ ] 4 skewers

Serves 4

tender SLICES   dainty TIDBITS

bite- sized CHUNKS

handy CRUSHED   refreshing JUICE

1. Cut ham into 1-inch cubes.

2. Drain pineapple chunks.

3. Wash green pepper and cut into 1-inch squares.

4. Thread skewers with green pepper, ham, and pineapple until skewer is full.

5. Broil several minutes until nicely browned. Serve on skewers or put pieces on dinner plates.

tutti fruity pork chops

- [ ] 4 thick pork chops
- [ ] garlic salt
- [ ] pepper
- [ ] 2 tbsps salad oil
- [ ] 1 8 oz. can crushed pineapple
- [ ] 1 cup (8 oz.) orange juice

Serves 4

Delight
SPECIAL DIETETIC PACK
Without added Sugar
DIETETIC FOODS

1. Heat oven to 350 degrees.

2. Sprinkle pork chops with garlic salt and pepper.

3. Heat oil in frying pan and brown chops 5 minutes on each side.

4. Arrange chops in a shallow baking dish.

5. Top each with a thick layer of pineapple and pour orange juice over all.

6. Bake 60 minutes. Remember to use oven mitts when removing dish from oven.

hamburger fake cake

- 1 1/2 pounds ground beef
- 1/4 cup frozen chopped onion
- 1/4 cup water
- 1 tsp salt
- 1 tsp soy sauce
- 1/4 tsp pepper
- instant mashed potatoes (enough for 4 servings)
- catsup and mustard (in squirt bottles, if possible)

Serves 4

1 Heat oven to 350 degrees.

2 With a fork, mix beef, onion, 1/4 cup water, 1 teaspoon salt, soy sauce, and pepper in a bowl.

3 Place beef mixture in an ungreased pie pan and shape into a mound (like a cake).

4 Bake 45 minutes.

5 Five minutes before the hamburger is done, prepare the instant mashed potatoes.

6 Remove hamburger from the oven. Remember to use oven mitts when removing pan from oven. Carefully lift to a platter with a pancake turner.

7 Frost with mashed potatoes using a staight-edged spatula.

8 Decorate the top with catsup and mustard.

side dishes and breads

chapter 3

french fried potatoes

1 32-oz. pkg frozen French fries

seasoning salt

1 Preheat oven to 450 degrees.

2 Spread frozen French fries on a baking sheet and place in oven; bake 15 to 20 minutes or until golden brown.

3 Using a oven mitt remove baking sheet from oven; pour potatoes onto a plate lined with a paper towel.

4 Sprinkle with seasoning salt and serve.

Salt

Serves 6 to 8

mashed potatoes

Serves 4 to 6

- ☐ **6 medium potatoes**
- ☐ **water**
- ☐ **2 1/4 tsps salt, divided**
- ☐ **1/2 cup milk**
- ☐ **3 tbsps butter**
- ☐ **parsley sprigs (optional)**

1 Wash and peel the potatoes; cut each one in half.

2 Place potato halves in a saucepan. Add enough water to cover; sprinkle 2 teaspoons salt over potatoes.

3 Cook over medium heat 20 to 25 minutes. Potatoes are done when a fork pierces them easily.

4 Drain potatoes in a wire strainer. CAUTION: Potatoes will be VERY hot.

5 In a large mixing bowl mash together cooked potatoes, milk, butter, and remaining 1/4 teaspoon salt. Beat until light and fluffy.

6 Spoon potatoes into serving dish and decorate with parsley, if desired.

cheese baked potatoes

 Preheat oven to 350 degrees.

2. Scrub the potatoes under running water to clean.

3. Rub each potato with butter.

4. Using a fork make steam vents by poking the potatoes all over.

5. Place the potatoes on the center rack of the oven and bake 1 1/2 hours.

6. CAUTION: Potatoes will be VERY hot! Using clean oven mitts remove potatoes from oven and put on a cutting board. Cut slits lengthwise on the potatoes. Scoop out the insides and put in a bowl. Be careful not to poke through or tear the skins.

7. Using a fork mash the potato insides well. Add cheese and mix well.

8. Preheat the broiler.

9. Spoon the mixture back into the potato skins; using a fork press down gently on the tops.

10. Broil until the tops are golden brown.

☐ **3 large potatoes**
☐ **butter**
☐ **1 cup cheddar cheese or other favorite cheese, grated**

Serves 4 to 6

baked potatoes

Serves 4

- [ ] **4 medium baking potatoes**
- [ ] **salad oil, if desired**
- [ ] **butter to taste**
- [ ] **salt and pepper to taste**

1 Preheat oven to 350 degrees.

2 Scrub the potatoes under running water to clean.

3 Rub each potato with salad oil if desired (it will make the skins softer).

4 Using a fork make steam vents by poking the potatoes all over.

5 Place the potatoes on the center rack of the oven and bake 1 1/2 hours.

6 CAUTION: Potatoes will be VERY hot! Using clean oven mitts remove potatoes from oven and put on a cutting board. Cut slits in the potatoes and squeeze each potato open.

7 Top with butter, salt, and pepper.

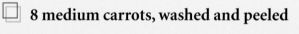

buttered carrot sticks

 8 medium carrots, washed and peeled

1 tsp salt

2 tbsps butter

1 On a cutting board, cut carrots into 1/2-inch strips.

2 Place carrots in a saucepan and cover with water.

3 Add salt and cover.

4 Cook over medium heat 18 to 20 minutes. Carrots are done when easily pierced with a fork.

5 Using a slotted spoon place carrots in a serving dish and top with butter.

Serves 4 to 6

bunny salad

- ☐ **4 crisp lettuce leaves**
- ☐ **4 chilled pear halves**
- ☐ **8 raisins**
- ☐ **4 red cinnamon candies**
- ☐ **8 blanched almonds**
- ☐ **1 cup cottage cheese**

1 Place a lettuce leaf on four small plates.

2 Lay a pear half with cut side down on top of each lettuce leaf.

3 Create a bunny face on the narrow end of the pear:

    Use raisins for eyes.

    Use cinnamon candy for nose.

    Use almonds for ears.

    Use 1 tablespoon cottage cheese for tail.

Serves 4

cheese-scalloped corn

Serves 4

- [ ] **1 15-oz. can cream-style corn**
- [ ] **2 eggs**
- [ ] **1/2 cup cheddar cheese, shredded**
- [ ] **1/2 tsp salt**
- [ ] **1/4 cup dry bread crumbs**

1 Heat oven to 350 degrees.

 2 In an ungreased casserole dish mix together corn, eggs, cheese, and salt.

 3 Sprinkle bread crumbs over the top.

 4 Bake 35 minutes. Remember to use oven mitts when removing dish from oven.

cheesy tomato-bean bake

Serves 4

- 1 14-1/2-oz. can green beans
- 2 medium tomatoes, washed and cored
- salt to taste
- 4 slices processed American cheese

1 Heat oven to 350 degrees.

2 Drain beans and place in an ungreased pie dish.

3 Slice tomatoes and lay over the beans.

 4 Sprinkle with a little salt.

 5 Cover with cheese.

 6 Bake 20 minutes. Remember to use oven mitts when removing dish from oven.

crunchy green beans

 1 Heat oven to 350 degrees.

 2 Drain green beans.

 3 In an ungreased casserole dish, mix beans with half the can of soup; cover.

4 Bake 20 minutes.

5 Using oven mitts, remove dish from oven and pour half the can of onions on top.

6 Bake uncovered 15 minutes.

☐ 1 14-1/2-oz. can French-style green beans

☐ 1 10-3/4-oz. can condensed cream of mushroom soup, divided (see Note)

☐ 1 6-oz. can French-fried onions, divided (see Note)

Serves 4

Note: Cover and refrigerate remaining soup to be used the next day. To cook, fill half the soup can with water or milk and heat as directed. Sprinkle remaining onions on top of the soup just before serving.

canned peas deluxe

☐ 1 14-1/2-oz. can of peas

☐ 1 tbsp butter

1 Pour liquid from peas into a saucepan.

2 Boil uncovered 2 to 3 minutes until liquid cooks down halfway.

3 Stir in butter.

4 Add peas and heat thoroughly.

Serves 4

tossed green salad

Ingredients:

- salad greens of your choice, such as iceberg, Bibb, or Boston lettuce
- celery
- radishes
- cucumbers
- tomatoes
- salt and pepper to taste
- 2 tbsps olive oil or vegetable oil
- 1 tbsp lemon juice

 1 Peel off as many lettuce leaves as you need, depending upon how many people you are serving.

 2 Wash leaves well under cold running water; pat dry with paper towel. If time allows, refrigerate leaves until ready for use.

3 Tear lettuce into bite-sized pieces and place in a salad bowl.

 4 Wash all vegetables under cold running water; be sure to scrub well.

5 On a chopping board slice radishes, cucumbers, and celery; cut tomatoes into wedges.

 6 Put cut vegetables on top of lettuce pieces. Sprinkle with salt and pepper.

 7 In a small cup or bowl mix together olive or vegetable oil and lemon juice; mix well.

 8 Sprinkle oil mixture over greens and toss.

garlic croutons

- ☐ **4 slices white bread**
- ☐ **butter, softened**
- ☐ **1/4 tsp garlic powder**

 Heat oven to 400 degrees.

 Trim crust from bread slices.

 Spread both sides of bread with butter.

Sprinkle with garlic powder.

 Cut into 1/2-inch squares and place on ungreased baking sheet.

 Bake 10 to 15 minutes or until golden brown and crisp, stirring occasionally.

Using oven mitts, remove baking sheet from oven and cool.

Store croutons in a tightly covered container and use on tossed green salad or soup.

fruit salad

- [ ] 1 banana, peeled and sliced
- [ ] 1 orange, peeled and sliced
  (remove any seeds)
- [ ] 1 pear, peeled, cored, and sliced
- [ ] a few grapes, halved
- [ ] a few cherries, pitted and halved
- [ ] 1/2 cup water
- [ ] 1/4 cup sugar

1 In a bowl toss together banana, orange, pear, grapes, and cherries.

2 In a saucepan mix water and sugar.

3 Bring to a boil and cook 2 minutes, stirring occasionally.

4 Pour over fruit and cool.

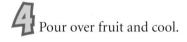

Serves 2

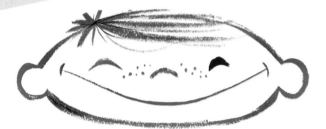

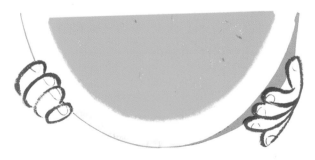

fruit kabobs

- ☐ **8 maraschino cherries**
- ☐ **8 pineapple chunks**
- ☐ **8 miniature marshmallows**
- ☐ **8 toothpicks**

1 On each toothpick skewer one cherry, one pineapple chunk, and one marshmallow.

2 Serve. Be sure not to bite the toothpick!

Serves 2

daisy salads

Serves 4

1. Wash lettuce leaf and pat dry with paper towel.

2. Wash celery stalk. Trim off leaves and set them aside.

3. Cut celery into thin 2-inch-long strips. Keep 4 strips for salads and refrigerate the rest.

4. Spoon 1/3 cup cottage cheese onto center of 4 salad plates. Put 1 peach half on top of cottage cheese mound, cut side up.

5. With scissors cut each marshmallow into 5 circles. (To keep the scissors from sticking, dip them in water before cutting.)

6. Pour a little sugar into a saucer and dip each side of the cut marshmallow pieces into the sugar.

7. Arrange the marshmallow circles around the edge of each peach half so they look like a flower.

8. Put a cherry in the center of each flower.

9. Use a strip of celery strip to make the stem. Place a few celery leaves along the side of the celery strip, if desired.

10. Tear the lettuce leaf into 4 strips and lay at the bottom of the stem to look like grass.

- ☐ 1 lettuce leaf
- ☐ 1 celery stalk with leaves
- ☐ 1 1/3 cups cottage cheese
- ☐ 4 canned peach halves, drained on paper towel
- ☐ 4 large marshmallows
- ☐ sugar
- ☐ 4 maraschino cherries, drained on paper towel

crunchy coleslaw

- [ ] 2 cups cabbage, chopped
- [ ] 1 medium red apple, washed, cored, cut into 1/4-inch pieces
- [ ] 1 cup miniature marshmallows
- [ ] 1 tsp bottled lemon juice
- [ ] 1/2 cup pineapple, lemon, or lime yogurt
- [ ] 2 tbsps chopped nuts

1 In a mixing bowl stir together cabbage, apple, and marshmallows.

2 Sprinkle lemon juice over top and blend in yogurt.

3 Top with nuts and serve.

Serves 4 to 5

monkey bread

- [ ] **4 cans refrigerated biscuits**
- [ ] **3/4 cup butter**
- [ ] **1 1/2 cups sugar, divided**
- [ ] **2 1/2 tsp cinnamon, divided**

why MONKEY AROUND?

Serves 6 to 8

1 Heat oven to 350 degrees.

2 Separate biscuits and cut each one into quarters; roll each quarter into a ball.

3 In a small bowl stir together 1/2 cup sugar and 1 teaspoon cinnamon.

4 Roll each ball in the sugar mixture.

5 Grease a bundt or angel food cake pan and drop in balls, keeping them even all around the pan.

6 In a small saucepan melt butter and blend in remaining 1 cup sugar and 1 1/2 teaspoons cinnamon.

7 Pour over biscuits and bake 45 minutes. Remember to use oven mitts when removing pan from oven.

8 Turn out of pan to serve. Note: There's no need to cut. Just pull off a biscuit at a time.

drop biscuits

- ☐ **2 cups flour, sifted**
- ☐ **3 tsps baking powder**
- ☐ **1 tsp salt**
- ☐ **1/3 cup shortening, softened**
- ☐ **3/4 cup milk**

1 Heat oven to 450 degrees.

2 In a bowl blend together flour, baking powder, and salt.

3 Using a fork cut in shortening until mixture is crumbly.

4 Stir in milk.

5 Using a rubber scraper and a spoon for scraping the bowl, drop spoonfuls of dough onto the baking sheet; leave about 2 inches between biscuits.

6 Bake 10 to 12 minutes or until brown. Remember to use oven mitts when removing baking sheet from oven.

Serves 4 to 6

cinnamon twists

- [ ] **2 tbsps butter**
- [ ] **1/4 cup sugar**
- [ ] **1 tsp ground cinnamon**
- [ ] **1 pkg refrigerated biscuits (8 biscuits)**
- [ ] **1 tbsp chopped walnuts**

 Heat oven to 425 degrees.

 In a small saucepan melt butter; remove from heat.

 In a small bowl blend together sugar and cinnamon.

 Using a ruler to measure, roll each biscuit into a 9-inch rope.

 Bring ends of ropes together and pinch to seal.

 Set ropes in the melted butter and flip to coat well; then dip in sugar-cinnamon mixture.

 Twist each rope once to form a figure 8 and place on baking sheet.

 Sprinkle nuts over the top of each figure 8.

9 Bake 8 to 10 minutes, remove with spatula, and cool on wire racks. Remember to use oven mitts when removing baking sheet from oven.

Makes 8 twists

banana nut bread

- [ ] **2 cups flour**
- [ ] **1/2 tsp baking soda**
- [ ] **1/2 tsp baking powder**
- [ ] **1/2 tsp salt**
- [ ] **1 cup sugar**
- [ ] **2 eggs**
- [ ] **3 very ripe bananas, mashed**
- [ ] **1/2 cup walnuts, chopped (optional)**

Help yourself—
GRABABANANA !

1 Heat oven to 350 degrees.

2 Grease and lightly flour a loaf pan.

3 In a bowl blend all ingredients together, stirring well.

4 Pour into the pan.

5 Bake 55 to 60 minutes or until a toothpick inserted comes out clean.
Remember to use oven mitts when removing pan from oven.

Serves 4 to 6

bread sticks

- ☐ 1 pkg 8 hot dog buns
- ☐ 1 pound butter, melted
- ☐ seasoning salt
- ☐ garlic salt
- ☐ Parmesan cheese
- ☐ dried parsley (or any kind of spice and herbs you like)

1 Heat oven to 350 degrees.

2 Keeping buns closed, cut each one into 3 equal strips lengthwise – 6 strips per bun.

3 Dunk strips into melted butter and arrange closely on a baking sheet.

4 Over each top sprinkle seasoning salt, garlic salt, Parmesan cheese, and dried parsley (or other spices and herbs).

5 Bake 10 to 15 minutes or until golden brown.

6 Turn off oven and keep bread sticks in oven several hours.

7 Remove from oven and lay on paper towels. Remember to use oven mitts when removing baking sheet from oven.

8 Store in a tightly covered container (they may also be frozen).

Serves 6 to 8

Note: These are great with soups, salads, and pasta.

dare to dessert

chapter 4

pudding cones

1. Shall we? Let's do!

2. Ooops, almost spilled the milk!

Be sure we get every bit of puddin' in . . .

And we can take turns spinning the beater!

5. Isn't it just d'licious?

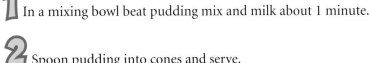

Serves 8

- ☐ **1 4-oz. package instant pudding (any flavor)**
- ☐ **2 cups milk**
- ☐ **8 ice cream cones**

Note: Place cones in a small glass when filling so they don't fall over.

1 In a mixing bowl beat pudding mix and milk about 1 minute.

2 Spoon pudding into cones and serve.

apple crisp

- [ ] **4 cups (4 medium) apples, peeled, cored, and sliced**
- [ ] **1/4 cup water**
- [ ] **1 tsp cinnamon**
- [ ] **1/2 tsp salt**
- [ ] **1 cup sugar**
- [ ] **3/4 cup flour**
- [ ] **1/3 cup butter, softened**

1 Heat oven to 350 degrees.

2 Evenly spread apples in an 8 x 8 x 2-inch square pan.

3 Over apples sprinkle water, cinnamon, and salt.

4 In a small bowl using a fork, blend together sugar, flour, and butter until crumbly.

5 Spread mixture over apples.

6 Bake uncovered 35 to 40 minutes. Remember to use oven mitts when removing pan from oven.

7 Serve warm with milk or cream.

Serves 6

AN APPLE
A DAY
Keeps the
DOCTOR
AWAY...

baked apples

- 6 apples, washed and cored
- 1/2 cup brown sugar, packed
- 1/2 tsp ground cinnamon
- 1 cup water

Serves 6

1 Heat oven to 350 degrees.

2 Using a potato peeler, peel a strip from around the top of each apple. Discard strip.

3 Place apples in a baking dish so that they are standing upright.

4 In a small bowl stir together brown sugar and cinnamon.

5 Fill each apple with sugar mixture.

6 Pour water around apples.

7 Cover and bake 55 to 60 minutes or until apples prick easily with a fork. Remember to use oven mitts when removing dish from oven.

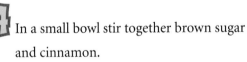

junior banana splits

- ☐ **4 bananas**
- ☐ **1 pint vanilla ice cream**
- ☐ **1 jar pineapple topping**
- ☐ **canned whipped topping**
- ☐ **4 maraschino cherries**

1 Peel the bananas; slice them lengthwise and then crosswise.

2 On a small flat dessert dish arrange each banana, cut ends in the middle, to resemble a plus sign: **+**.

3 Put a scoop of ice cream in the center of the banana.

4 Spoon on the pineapple topping, add whipped topping, and dot with a cherry.

Serves 4

crispy crackolates

- 2 1/2 tbsps sugar
- 1 tbsp butter
- 4 tbsps cocoa
- 1 tbsp light corn syrup
- 9 tbsps cornflakes

1 In a saucepan stir together sugar, butter, cocoa, and corn syrup.

2 Over low heat slowly melt the ingredients; be sure they do not boil.

3 Remove from heat and cool slightly.

4 Fold in cornflakes and stir gently until well coated.

5 Using a spoon scoop mixture onto waxed paper or a plate and make small piles; let set. Eat when cool.

COOKIES

HiYA, COOKIE!

Serves 2 to 4

five-minute fudge

- [ ] 1 6-oz. can evaporated milk
- [ ] 1 2/3 cups sugar
- [ ] 1/2 tsp salt
- [ ] 1 tsp vanilla
- [ ] 1/2 cup chopped walnuts
- [ ] 1 1/2 cups miniature marshmallows
- [ ] 1 1/2 cups semisweet chocolate bits

WALNUTS work wonde

 Grease a 9 x 9 x 2-inch square pan.

 In a medium saucepan stir together evaporated milk, sugar, and salt.

 Heat to just boiling (do not boil); reduce heat and simmer 5 minutes.

 Remove from heat; stir in vanilla, walnuts, marshmallows, and chocolate bits; mix until smooth.

 Pour into pan. Cut into squares when cool.

Serves 4 to 6

fruit crumble

Serves 4 to 6

- [ ] 1 pound fruit (apples, plums, rhubarb, etc.)
- [ ] 1/2 cup plus 2 tbsps sugar, divided
- [ ] 1/4 to 1/2 cup water
- [ ] 1 1/2 cups self-raising flour
- [ ] pinch of salt
- [ ] 3 tbsps butter

1 Heat oven to 400 degrees.

2 Wash all the fruit. If needed, peel, core, or pit fruit. Cut into small pieces.

3 Place fruit in a pie dish and sprinkle 1/2 cup sugar over the top.

4 Add 1/4 cup water (1/2 cup water if using only apples). Set aside.

5 In a small bowl blend together flour and salt. Using a fork, cut in butter until crumbly.

6 Add remaining 2 tablespoons sugar and mix thoroughly.

7 Spread the crumble mixture evenly over the fruit.

8 Bake 30 minutes in the top half of the oven. Test with skewer to see if fruit is soft. Bake another 10 minutes if needed. Remember to use oven mitts when removing dish from oven.

baked bananas

- ☐ **butter**
- ☐ **bananas (1 per person)**
- ☐ **brown sugar**
- ☐ **heavy cream**

1 Grease a baking dish with butter.

2 Heat oven to 350 degrees.

3 Peel bananas and cut in half lengthwise; set in baking dish.

4 Sprinkle sugar over bananas.

5 Bake 10 minutes. Remember to use oven mitts when removing dish from oven.

6 In a small bowl beat cream until thick and fluffy.

7 Serve bananas topped with cream.

Makes 1 banana per person

94

tropical treat

☐ **1 8-oz. can mandarin oranges, chilled and drained**

☐ **1 8-oz. can pineapple tidbits, chilled and drained**

☐ **1/2 cup miniature marshmallows**

☐ **1 pint heavy cream, whipped**

1 In a large bowl mix together oranges, pineapple, and marshmallows.

2 Add enough whipped cream to cover the fruit, stir gently, and serve.

porcupines

Serves 6 to 8

☐ **1 cup creamy peanut butter**

☐ **1/2 cup sweetened condensed milk**

☐ **1/4 cup powdered sugar**

☐ **1/2 cup salted peanuts, finely chopped**

1 In a bowl combine peanut butter, condensed milk, and powdered sugar; mix well and knead with your hands until mixture is thoroughly blended.

2 Divide mixture into about 24 balls 1 inch in diameter.

3 Roll each ball in chopped peanuts. Can be chilled before serving.

easy chocolate chippers

- 1 pkg 2-layer yellow cake mix
- 1/4 cup butter, softened
- 1/3 cup milk
- 1 egg
- 1 cup semisweet chocolate bits
- 1/2 cup walnuts, chopped

1 Lightly grease a baking sheet.

2 Heat oven to 375 degrees.

3 In a bowl blend together cake mix, butter, milk, and egg; stir well.

4 Fold in chocolate bits and walnuts.

5 Using a teaspoon, drop dough onto baking sheet about 2 inches apart.

6 Bake 10 to 12 minutes. Remember to use oven mitts when removing baking sheet from oven.

7 Remove cookies with spatula and cool on wire racks.

Makes 2 dozen

sparkling sugar cookies

1 Heat oven to 400 degrees.

2 In a bowl mix together shortening, 1 cup sugar, and lemon peel.

3 Blend in egg and milk; beat well.

4 In another bowl stir together flour, baking powder, salt, and baking soda.

5 Add dry ingredients to the shortening mixture; blend well.

6 Using a teaspoon drop dough onto baking sheet about 2 inches apart.

- [ ] 1/2 cup shortening, softened
- [ ] 1 cup sugar, plus additional for dipping
- [ ] 1 tsp lemon peel, grated
- [ ] 1 egg
- [ ] 2 tbsps milk
- [ ] 2 cups flour
- [ ] 1 tsp baking powder
- [ ] 1/2 tsp salt
- [ ] 1/2 tsp baking soda

Makes 3 dozen

7 Grease the bottom of a glass and dip in sugar. Flatten each cookie with the glass, dipping bottom in sugar each time you flatten.

8 Bake 8 to 10 minutes or until golden brown. Remember to use oven mitts when removing baking sheet from oven.

9 Remove cookies with a spatula and cool on wire racks.

stir-n-drop oatmeal cookies

- ☐ 1 cup flour
- ☐ 1 tsp baking powder
- ☐ 1/2 tsp salt
- ☐ 1/2 tsp cinnamon
- ☐ 1/2 tsp ginger
- ☐ 1 cup brown sugar, packed
- ☐ 1 cup rolled oats
- ☐ 1/4 cup vegetable oil
- ☐ 2 tbsps milk
- ☐ 1 egg
- ☐ 3/4 cup walnuts, chopped (optional)

Makes 3 dozen

1 Heat oven to 375 degrees.

2 In a bowl combine flour, baking powder, salt, cinnamon, and ginger.

3 Stir in brown sugar and oats.

4 Mix in oil, milk, and egg; blend well.

5 Stir in walnuts, if using.

6 Using a teaspoon drop dough onto baking sheet about 2 inches apart.

7 Bake 8 to10 minutes. Remember to use oven mitts when removing baking sheet from oven.

8 Remove cookies with a spatula and cool on wire racks.

quick peanut butter cookies

- [ ] 1 pkg yellow cake mix, divided
- [ ] 1 cup chunky peanut butter
- [ ] 2 eggs
- [ ] 1/3 cup water
- [ ] flour

Makes 4 to 5 dozen

1 Heat oven to 375 degrees.

2 In a large bowl blend together 1/2 package cake mix, peanut butter, eggs, and water; beat until smooth.

3 Mix in remaining 1/2 package cake mix; stir thoroughly, using your hands if necessary.

4 Using a teaspoon drop dough onto baking sheet about 3 inches apart. Use a fork dipped in flour to flatten dough making a crisscross design on top of each cookie.

5 Bake 8 to 10 minutes or until golden brown. Remember to use oven mitts when removing baking sheet from oven.

6 Cool cookies on baking sheet about 2 minutes before removing to cool on wire racks.

pick-your-flavor cookies

- [ ] 1 16 1/2-oz. can frosting, any flavor, divided
- [ ] 2 cups biscuit baking mix
- [ ] 1 egg

Makes 2 to 3 dozen

1 Grease baking sheet.

2 Heat oven to 375 degrees.

3 Measure 3/4 cup frosting; set the rest aside.

4 In a bowl mix baking mix, egg, and 3/4 cup frosting; dough will be stiff.

5 Using a teaspoon drop dough onto baking sheet about 2 inches apart.

6 Bake 10 to 12 minutes or until cookie springs back when touched. Remember to use oven mitts when removing baking sheet from oven.

7 Remove cookies with a spatula and cool on wire racks.

8 Spread remaining frosting over cooled cookies.

- ☐ 1 cup flour
- ☐ 1 cup quick-cooking oats, uncooked
- ☐ 1/2 cup sugar
- ☐ 1/2 cup brown sugar, firmly packed
- ☐ 1/2 tsp baking soda
- ☐ 1/3 cup peanut butter, chunky or smooth
- ☐ 1/2 cup butter
- ☐ 1 egg, slightly beaten
- ☐ frosting (see right)

peanut butter bar cookies

1. Grease a rectangle baking pan.

2. Heat oven to 350 degrees.

Makes 24 squares

3. In a mixing bowl blend together flour, oats, sugars, baking soda, peanut butter, and butter.

4. Add egg to mixture; mix until crumbly.

5. Press mixture firmly into pan.

6. Bake on center rack 20 to 25 minutes or until a toothpick inserted comes out clean. Remember to use oven mitts when removing pan from oven.

7. Spread frosting over cooled cookies; cut into 2-inch squares.

frosting

- ☐ 1 16 1/2-oz. can vanilla frosting
- ☐ 1/4 cup peanut butter

1. In a small bowl beat together 1/2 can frosting and peanut butter.

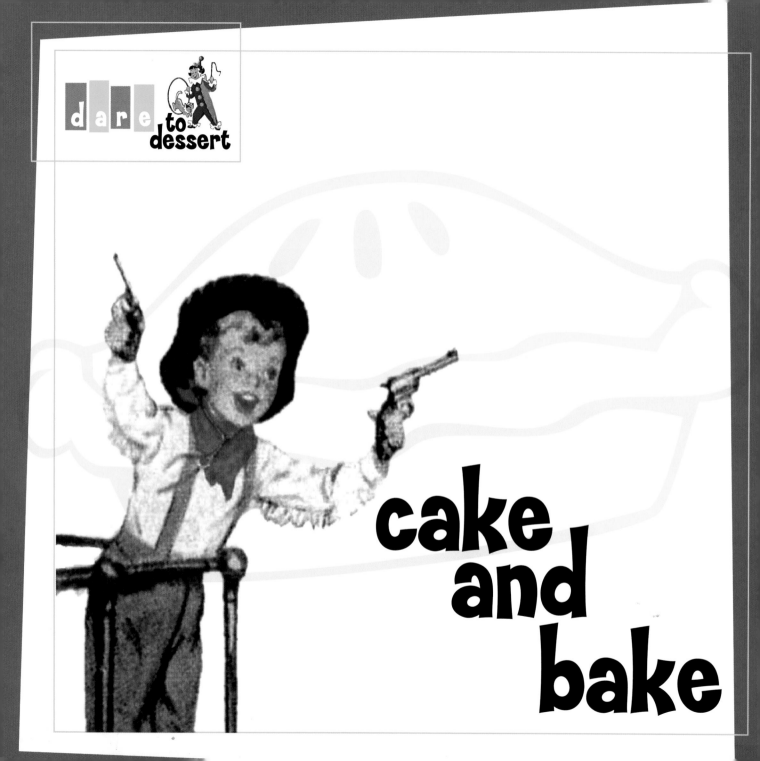

peanut butter cupcakes

- [ ] 1/4 cup brown sugar, packed
- [ ] 1 1/2 cups flour, sifted and divided
- [ ] 2 tbsps peanut butter
- [ ] 1 tbsp butter, melted
- [ ] 1/2 tsp ground cinnamon
- [ ] 1/3 cup shortening
- [ ] 1/2 cup sugar
- [ ] 1 tsp vanilla
- [ ] 1 egg
- [ ] 1 1/2 tsps baking powder
- [ ] 1/4 tsp salt
- [ ] 1/2 cup milk
- [ ] 12 paper baking cups

Makes 1 dozen

1. Heat oven to 375 degrees.

2. In a small bowl blend together brown sugar, 1/4 cup flour, peanut butter, butter, and cinnamon; mix until crumbly. Set aside to use as topping.

3. In another bowl cream together shortening, sugar, and vanilla; beat until fluffy and creamy. Add egg and beat well.

4. In separate bowl sift together remaining 1 1/4 cups flour, baking powder, and salt.

5. Alternately add flour mixture and milk to creamed mixture, beating well after each addition.

6. Line muffin pans with paper baking cups and fill half full.

7. Sprinkle peanut butter mixture over top.

8. Bake 20 minutes. Remember to use oven mitts when removing muffin pans from oven.

crunchy peach cobbler

Serves 6 to 8

- [ ] 6 fresh peaches, peeled, pitted, and sliced
- [ ] 1 cup sugar
- [ ] 2 tbsps lemon juice
- [ ] 1 14-oz. pkg oatmeal muffin mix
- [ ] 1/4 tsp ground nutmeg
- [ ] 1/2 cup butter, softened

1 Heat oven to 375 degrees.

2 In a bowl combine peach slices, sugar, and lemon juice.

3 Pour into a square baking dish.

4 In a bowl blend together muffin mix and nutmeg.

5 Using a fork mix in butter until crumbly.

6 Sprinkle mixture over peaches.

7 Bake 40 to 45 minutes. Remember to use oven mitts when removing dish from oven.

8 Cut into squares and serve warm with ice cream.

blueberry cobbler

- ☐ 1 13 1/2-oz. pkg blueberry muffin mix
- ☐ 1 21-oz. can blueberry pie filling
- ☐ 1 tbsp bottled lemon juice
- ☐ 1 tsp cinnamon
- ☐ 1 egg
- ☐ 1/2 cup milk
- ☐ vanilla ice cream (optional)

1 Heat oven to 400 degrees.

2 Open the can of blueberries in the muffin mix package and drain in a strainer over a saucepan; set blueberries aside.

3 Add pie filling, lemon juice, and cinnamon to the blueberry liquid in saucepan; stir well.

4 Heat to just boiling, then pour into an ungreased rectangle-shaped baking pan.

5 Rinse the blueberries and drain.

6 Prepare the muffin mix batter as directed using the blueberries. Spread over hot pie filling mixture.

7 Bake 25 to 30 minutes. Remember to use oven mitts when removing pan from oven.

8 Top each serving with a scoop of ice cream, if desired.

Serves 6 to 8

cheery cherry cobbler

1 Heat oven to 375 degrees.

2 Separate biscuits and put them on an ungreased baking sheet a few inches apart.

3 Brush top of each biscuit with melted butter.

4 In a small bowl combine sugar and cinnamon; sprinkle over biscuits.

5 Bake 12 to 15 minutes or until golden brown. Remember to use oven mitts when removing baking sheet from oven.

6 In a saucepan heat pie filling.

7 To serve, place one biscuit in a small bowl and spoon pie filling over.

8 Top each serving with a scoop of ice cream, if desired.

- [ ] 1 pkg refrigerated biscuits
- [ ] 2 tbsps butter, melted
- [ ] 2 tbsps sugar
- [ ] 1/2 tsp cinnamon
- [ ] 1 21-oz. can cherry pie filling
- [ ] vanilla ice cream (optional)

Serves 6 to 8

brownies

- ☐ 1 egg
- ☐ 1 cup chocolate syrup
- ☐ 1/2 cup butter
- ☐ 1 cup flour
- ☐ 1/2 cup sugar
- ☐ 1/2 tsp salt
- ☐ 1/2 cup chopped nuts

GIVE YOUR CHILD EXTRA IRON IN DELICIOUS FOODS

1 Grease a 9 x 9 x 2-inch square pan.

2 Heat oven to 350 degrees.

Serves 6 to 8

3 In a bowl blend together egg, syrup, and butter; beat well until smooth.

4 In another bowl sift together flour, sugar, and salt. Add the dry mixture to the chocolate mixture and stir in nuts.

5 Pour batter into the pan.

6 Bake 30 minutes. Remember to use oven mitts when removing pan from oven.

7 Cool and cut into squares.

cocoa fudge cake

- ☐ **1 3/4 cups flour**
- ☐ **1 1/3 cups sugar**
- ☑ **6 tbsps cocoa**
- ☐ **1 tsp baking soda**
- ☐ **1 tsp salt**
- ☐ **1/2 cup shortening, softened**
- ☐ **1 cup buttermilk**
- ☐ **1 tsp vanilla**
- ☐ **3 eggs**
- ☐ **frosting (see below)**

1 Grease and flour a 13 x 9 1/2-inch rectangle baking pan.

2 Heat oven to 350 degrees.

3 In a bowl combine flour, sugar, cocoa, baking soda, and salt.

4 Beat in shortening, buttermilk, and vanilla; beat at least 2 minutes.

5 Add in eggs and beat 2 minutes.

6 Pour batter into pan.

7 Bake 40 to 45 minutes. Remember to use oven mitts when removing pan from oven.

8 Cool in pan on a wire rack and frost.

frosting

- ☐ **1 cup sugar**
- ☐ **1/4 cup cocoa**
- ☐ **1/4 cup butter**
- ☐ **1/2 cup milk**
- ☐ **2 tbsps light corn syrup**
- ☐ **1 1/2 cups powdered sugar, sifted**
- ☐ **1 tsp vanilla**

1 In a saucepan combine sugar and cocoa; blend in butter, milk, and corn syrup.

2 Bring to a boil and cook 3 minutes, stirring occasionally.

3 Remove from heat and set bottom of pan in cold water.

4 When bottom of pan is just warm, stir in powdered sugar and vanilla.

5 Beat frosting until thick enough to spread.

Note: Frosting can be thinned with milk or thickened with powdered sugar, as needed.

Serves 6 to 8

strawberry shortcake

1 Heat oven to 450 degrees.

2 In a bowl blend together biscuit mix, sugar, milk, and butter; beat well.

3 Turn out on a lightly floured board and knead 8 to 10 times.

Serves 6 to 8

4 Separate dough into halves. With floured hands pat half the dough into a greased round cake pan.

5 Dot with butter.

6 Roll the other half into a circle the size of the cake pan; place on top of the pan.

7 Bake 15 to 20 minutes or until golden brown. Remember to use oven mitts when removing pan from oven.

8 Remove shortcake from pan while warm and split crosswise to serve.

9 Spoon fresh strawberries over bottom portion; cover with top portion and add more strawberries.

10 Serve warm with whipped cream, if desired.

- ☐ **2 cups powdered biscuit mix**
- ☐ **2 tbsps sugar**
- ☐ **1/2 cup milk**
- ☐ **1/4 cup butter, melted**
- ☐ **2 tsps butter**
- ☐ **1 quart fresh strawberries**
- ☐ **whipped cream (optional)**

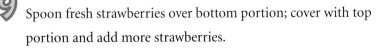

funny-face cupcakes

- [ ] **paper baking cups**
- [ ] **1 pkg cake mix, any flavor**
- [ ] **frosting (see below)**
- [ ] **raisins, almonds, or any other decoration**

1 Place paper cups in muffin tins.

2 Heat oven to 375 degrees. Prepare and bake cupcakes as directed on package.

Serves 6 to 8

3 Using oven mitts, remove pans from oven and turn cupcakes onto wire racks to cool.

4 Frost and decorate to make faces or any creation desired.

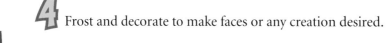

frosting

- [ ] **1/4 cup butter, softened**
- [ ] **1 3/4 cups powdered sugar, sifted and divided**
- [ ] **2 to 3 tbsps milk**
- [ ] **1 tsp vanilla**

1 In a small bowl cream together butter and 1 cup powdered sugar.

2 Gradually add remaining 3/4 cup powdered sugar, alternating with milk and vanilla; beat well.

- 1 1/3 cups flour
- 1 cup sugar
- 3 tbsps cocoa
- 1 tsp baking soda
- 1/2 tsp salt
- 6 tbsps vegetable oil
- 1 tbsp vinegar
- 1 tbsp vanilla
- 1 cup cold water
- whipped cream or powdered sugar

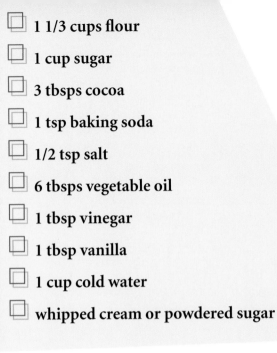

Serves 6 to 8

wacky cake

1 Grease a rectangle baking pan.

2 Heat oven to 375 degrees.

3 Place a piece of wax paper under a flour sifter.

4 Carefully place flour, sugar, cocoa, baking soda, and salt into the sifter.

5 Sift ingredients directly into baking pan.

6 Make three evenly spaced holes in dry ingredients.

7 Pour vegetable oil into the first hole, vinegar into the second hole, and vanilla into the third hole.

8 Pour water over the top.

9 Stir with a fork or whisk until well blended. Be sure to scrape the sides of the pan frequently.

10 Bake 50 to 60 minutes or until a toothpick inserted comes out clean.

11 Serve warm topped with whipped cream or powdered sugar.

swizzles and sips

drinks that chill

fruit float

☐ fruit (raspberries, blueberries, banana slices, strawberries, or any fruit you like)

☐ 8 oz. chilled ginger ale

☐ 1 scoop lime sherbet

1 Fill a tall glass with fruit.

2 Pour in ginger ale just to top of glass.

3 Top with lime sherbet.

Serves 1

root beer float

☐ 1 scoop vanilla ice cream

☐ 8 oz. chilled root beer

1 Put scoop of ice cream in a tall glass.

2 Fill glass with root beer.

blushing pink soda

- 2 tbsps strawberries, crushed
- 2 tbsps canned pineapple, crushed
- 2 tbsps vanilla ice cream
- 1/4 cup chilled strawberry soda

1 In a tall glass mix strawberries, pineapple, and ice cream.

2 Slowly pour in strawberry soda; stir. Top with additional ice cream or fruit.

Serves 1

orange fizz

- ☐ **1 cup orange juice**
- ☐ **1/4 cup sugar**
- ☐ **ice cubes**
- ☐ **2 7-oz. bottles chilled ginger ale**
- ☐ **orange slices, quartered**

1 In a jar or small bowl combine orange juice and sugar; chill.

2 Fill 4 tall glasses with ice cubes.

3 Add 1/4 cup chilled orange juice mixture to each glass.

4 Slowly fill glasses with ginger ale and gently stir.

5 Garnish with orange slices.

Serves 4

119

bouncing ball punch

- [ ] 1 46-oz. bottle fruit punch drink, any flavor
- [ ] 1 6-oz. can frozen lemonade concentrate
- [ ] 12 oz. water
- [ ] 3 10-oz. pkgs frozen melon balls

1 In a punch bowl mix fruit punch drink, lemonade concentrate, and water (fill the lemonade can twice).

2 Add melon balls and let stand 15 minutes.

3 Stir and serve.

Serves 15 to 20

banana smoothie shake

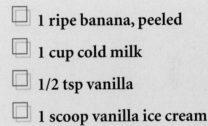

- [ ] **1 ripe banana, peeled**
- [ ] **1 cup cold milk**
- [ ] **1/2 tsp vanilla**
- [ ] **1 scoop vanilla ice cream**

1 In a bowl mash the banana with a fork.

2 Beat in milk and vanilla; mix well.

3 Pour into a tall glass and top with ice cream.

Serves 1

121

snow day warmers

Serves 6 to 8

cocoa

☐ **1/3 cup sugar**
☐ **1/3 cup cocoa**
☐ **1/4 tsp salt**
☐ **1 1/2 cups water**
☐ **4 1/2 cups milk**
☐ **1/4 tsp vanilla**

1 In a saucepan combine sugar, cocoa, and salt; add water.

2 Stirring constantly, heat to boiling; cook and stir 2 minutes.

3 Stir in milk; heat through (do not boil).

4 Add vanilla.

5 Stir until smooth and serve while hot.

Vitamins without coaxing!

spiced punch

Serves 6 to 8

- ☐ **1/4 cup lemon juice**
- ☐ **1 quart apple cider or apple juice**
- ☐ **cheese cloth or clean white cloth and string**
- ☐ **1 tsp ground cloves**
- ☐ **1 tsp ground nutmeg**
- ☐ **2 cinnamon sticks, broken into small pieces**

1 In a saucepan mix lemon juice with apple cider or juice.

2 Cut a 5 x 5-inch square out of cheesecloth or cloth. Place cloves, nutmeg, and broken cinnamon sticks on the cloth. Using string, tie cloth ends together to make a bag.

3 Place saucepan over low heat. Heat to boiling point and add bag of spices. Lower heat and simmer 5 to 10 minutes. Use tongs to remove bag of spices.

4 May be served hot or cold.

party punch

- [ ] 15 tea bags
- [ ] 3 cups boiling water
- [ ] 2/3 cup sugar
- [ ] 1 quart cold water
- [ ] 2 cups orange juice
- [ ] 1 cup bottled lemon juice
- [ ] ice cubes (optional)
- [ ] 1 1/2 quarts (1 quart plus 1 pint) ginger ale (optional)

Serves 15 to 20

1 Place tea bags in large saucepan and pour in boiling water; cover and let stand 4 minutes.

2 Use tongs to remove tea bags.

3 Stir in sugar until dissolved.

4 Add cold water, orange juice, and lemon juice.

5 Just before serving, pour into punch bowl.

6 May also be served cold with ice and ginger ale.

index

Side Dishes & Breads

Dare To Dessert

Swift & Sweet